1. The shed was hot _____

        from the sun

        ran to Nat

        in the chill

2. The box had shells _____.

        with a shop

        on its lid

        backpack in the fog

3. At Grandma and Grandpa's, Jan _____.

        lots to look at

        missed Mom and Dad

        and Dan

Use after page 12 of Unit 1. **Phrase Comprehension:** Have pupils read the first sentence and decide which of the three phrases below it makes sense in the sentence. Have them circle the correct phrase and write it in the sentence. Repeat for the remaining sentences having pupils work independently.

1

1. Dan had fun at Grandma and Grandpa's. ☐

2. Grandpa and Jan looked for Nat on the path in the woods. ☐

3. The shed was in the woods. ☐

4. Nat was on a mat on the path. ☐

5. The woodshed was locked. ☐

6. Dan yelled for Grandma to let them into the shed. ☐

7. Nat had catnip in the shed with him. ☐

8. Grandma was hot in the shed. ☐

Use after page 12 of Unit 1. **Recalling Details:** Pupils should carefully read the story beginning on page 6 before doing this exercise. Then have pupils read the first sentence and decide whether it is true or false. If it is true, have them put an **X** in the box. Repeat for the remaining sentences having pupils work independently.

1. Kim's <u>mom</u> has a shop.

   _____ shop has ships, shells, and books.

   His   Her   Its

2. Jan sees a ship with <u>a</u> <u>little</u> <u>cot</u>.

   _____ is on the deck of the ship.

   It   His   Its

3. "Can this <u>ship</u> go in the tub?" said Jan.

   "Yes, _____ can," said Kim's mom.

   her   them   it

4. Jan said, "Then I will get the ship for <u>Dan</u>."

   "He will have it for _____ bath," she said.

   her   it   his

5. Kim's mom said, "That will be good for <u>Dan</u>."

   "_____ will be happy with this ship," she said.

   Me   He   She

Use after page 12 of Unit 1. **Pronoun Referents:** Have pupils read the first sentence in the first exercise. Then have pupils read the second sentence and decide which of the three words below it could be placed in the blank to make the second sentence relate to the first. Have pupils circle the correct word and write it in the second sentence. Repeat for the remaining exercises having pupils work independently.

1. "I get fed well at my house," said Tam.

2. "Did you fill the shed with wood chips?" said Grandpa.

3. Jan said, "Nat was shut in the woodshed."

4. Gus said to Dan, "Can you shop with me?"

5. Jim said, "Do figs have shells?"

6. "Is a shack as little as a shed?" said Pam.

7. "Did you check the van yet?" said Grandma.

8. Kim said to her mom, "The house is in back of his."

9. "Grandma and Grandpa's house is so little on this map, Dan!" said Jan.

10. Dan said, "Jan, it looks as little as a bug."

Use after page 12 of Unit 1. **Punctuation:** Have pupils read the first sentence and draw a line under the speaker's exact words. Repeat for the remaining sentences having pupils work independently.

1. If Grandpa has to have books,   _____ Dan will set the box back.

2. If the lid will not fit,   _____ Dad will be happy.

3. If Dan gets a box for Dad,   _____ they will go with Grandpa.

4. If Jan and Dan have to shop,   _____ he will go to a book shop.

---

1. If Dan hugs the dogs in the shop,   _____ it is a good shop.

2. If Dan can fix the latch,   _____ Grandpa will be happy.

3. If the shop has lots,   _____ Rags is missed.

4. If he gets his books,   _____ he will get the box.

Use after page 12 of Unit 1. **Cause and Effect:** Pupils should carefully read the story beginning on page 9 before doing this exercise. Then have pupils read the first phrase. Have them decide which phrase on the right could be a result of the first phrase. Then have pupils write the number **1** on the line next to the correct phrase. Repeat for the remaining phrases having pupils work independently.

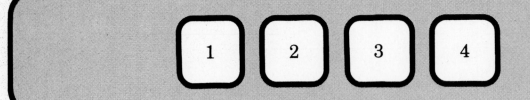

☐ Pam said to Dan and Jan, "Can you go back with us?"

1 Gus and Pam got to Grandpa and Grandma's.

☐ Grandpa and Grandma said that Jan and Dan can go with Pam.

☐ Jan and Dan pack the bags and go with Pam and Gus.

Use after page 18 of Unit 2. **Arranging Events in Sequence:** Pupils should carefully read the story beginning on page 15 before doing this exercise. Then have pupils read all of the sentences on this page. Have them find the number **1** and read the sentence that tells what happened first. Then have them decide which event happened next and write the number **2** in the correct box. Repeat for the remaining sentences having pupils work independently. Notice that the last one is also done for the pupils. Pupils may copy the sentences in correct sequence on a separate sheet of paper.

1. "Let us get a shell," said Dan.

   _____

2. Pam said, "That is a little house!"

   _____

3. The vans do not have kids in them.

   _____

4. Ben is with Gus in this van.

   _____

5. Pam cannot see the woodshed.

   _____

6. "It is wet in this tub," said Pam.

   _____

| can't | that's | let's | it's | don't | Ben's |

Use after page 18 of Unit 2. **Contractions:** Have pupils read the first sentence and decide which contraction at the bottom of the page could be substituted for the underlined words in the sentence. Have them rewrite the sentence on the line provided, using the correct contraction. Have pupils cross out the contractions at the bottom of the page as they use them. Repeat for the remaining sentences having pupils work independently.

1. It is very hot in the shed.

   _____?

2. The shop was filled with shells.

   _____?

3. Tam and Pam will backpack into the hills.

   _____?

4. Rags can lick her back.

   _____?

5. Jan will go back with Gus and Pam.

   _____?

6. Dan has missed his mom and dad.

   _____?

Use after page 18 of Unit 2. **Interrogative Transformations:** Have pupils read the first sentence. Then have them rearrange the words so that the sentence is asking something rather than telling something. Have pupils write the rearranged words on the line provided. Repeat for the remaining sentences having pupils work independently.

1. Kim's mom can catch a _____ for Nat.

    fish   hash   fig

2. Pam said, "_____, will you go to the shop with us?"

    cash   Dad   dish

3. The kids went on a _____ with Gus and Pam.

    mash   cash   trip

4. Do you have your _____ packed?

    bath   wish   bag

5. We have _____ to shop for a bed.

    shells   cash   jacks

6. Are you sick if you have a _____?

    rash   chin   book

Use after page 18 of Unit 2. **Sentence Comprehension:** Have pupils read the first sentence and decide which of the three words below it makes sense in the sentence. Have them circle the correct word and write it in the sentence. Repeat for the remaining sentences having pupils work independently.

9

1.   At the ranch Little Bud will run in the woods.
Jim and Kim will look in logs for bugs. And Mom
will forget her job.

Jim and Kim look for bugs.

Mom, Jim, and Kim will have fun at the ranch.

A run in the woods is fun.

2.   Pam's little ship had a chip in it. So she and Gus
took it in the van to a wood shop. The shop fixed the
ship and did a good job.

Gus did not fix Pam's ship.

Pam took her ship in the van.

The wood shop can fix ships.

3.   Dan looked in lots of cookbooks. He filled the
pot with yams and cooked them. Then he mashed
them. The Bells said that Dan was a good cook.

Dan can cook good yams.

The pots got filled with yams.

Mashed yams are a good lunch.

Use after page 18 of Unit 2. **Main Idea:** Have pupils read the first paragraph. Then have them read the three
sentences below the paragraph and decide which one tells the main idea of the paragraph. Have them circle the
correct sentence. Repeat for the remaining paragraphs having pupils work independently.

10

1. Pam fell into a ditch.

   She got mud on her socks.

   Pam _____.

                    sang a song

                    was sad

                    was happy

2. Kim sees a shell box.

   Tam has a ship in a jug.

   Kim and Tam are _____.

                    at a shop

                    in a rut

                    on a log

3. The kids go to the deck to see the sky.

   But the fog fills the sky.

   They can _____.

                    get a tan

                    look at the sun

                    look at TV

Use after page 24 of Unit 3. **Making Inferences to Draw Conclusions:** Have pupils read the first two sentences and decide which of the three phrases below them makes sense in the third sentence. Have them circle the correct phrase and write it in the third sentence. Repeat for the remaining sentences having pupils work independently.

11

1. Did the kids forget Nat was in <u>the</u> <u>shed</u>?

   He was not in _____ very long.

   they   his   it

2. But <u>Nat</u> had no cat mix in the shed.

   _____ did not get fed.

   It   He   Them

3. <u>The</u> <u>doctor</u> said that Nat was sick.

   _____ said, "Nat has a chill."

   It   They   She

4. "He will have lots of cat mix," said <u>Jan</u> <u>and</u> <u>Dan</u>.
   "_____ will get it for him," they said.

   They   Her   We

5. <u>Nat</u> will be fed.
   And _____ will get well.

   she   he   him

Use after page 24 of Unit 3. **Pronoun Referents:** Have pupils read the first sentence in the first exercise. Then have pupils read the second sentence and decide which of the three words below it could be placed in the blank to make the second sentence relate to the first. Have pupils circle the correct word and write it in the second sentence. Repeat for the remaining exercises having pupils work independently.

12

1. Jan hums a song _____ .

            in Gus's van

            with Kim and Jim

            on the bus

2. In the van Gus tells _____ .

            of a fish

            of a locked shed

            of a boy and his long trip in a ship

3. Gus's van ran _____ .

            into a TV

            into a ditch

            into a van

Use after page 24 of Unit 3. **Recalling Details:** Pupils should carefully read the story beginning on page 20 before doing this exercise. Then have the pupils read the first sentence and decide which of the phrases following the sentence is the most accurate. Have pupils circle the correct answer and write the phrase in the sentence. Repeat for the remaining sentences having pupils work independently.

13

top	got	rut
_____	_____	_____
_____	_____	_____
_____	_____	_____
_____	_____	_____
_____	_____	_____
_____	_____	_____

shut	hot	cot
chop	mop	shot
cut	hut	hop
dot	pot	shop
but	pop	

Use after page 24 of Unit 3. **Classifying Words by Patterns:** Have pupils find the words at the bottom of the page that belong in the first column. Have them write the words on the lines in the first column and cross them out at the bottom of the page as they use them. Repeat for the remaining columns having pupils work independently. Each word will be used only once.

1. Jim had _____ for his lunch than Kim.

2. Jan sang a _____ song for her mom.

3. Dan got his wish for a _____ box with a lid.

4. Nat was locked in _____ woodshed.

5. Are the _____ yams hot?

6. Grandpa said, "Rags is a good _____!"

7. Nat is a _____ cat.

8. "Did you forget the _____ buns for lunch?" said Dad.

less	fat	tin	mashed
six	Grandma's	long	dog

Use after page 24 of Unit 3. **Adjectives:** Have pupils read the first sentence. Then have them decide which word in the box at the bottom of the page makes sense in the sentence. Have pupils write the correct word in the sentence and cross it out at the bottom of the page. Repeat for the remaining sentences having pupils work independently. Answers may vary. Accept all reasonable answers.

1. rash
cash
rang

2. song
lock
long

3. spot
shot
shut

4.* for
from
house

5. rang
sang
sack

6.† shells
sheds
shacks

7. wish
will
fish

8. shop
shell
shed

9. ship
shut
shop

10. rang
rash
hang

11. ship
cut
shut

12. mash
cash
caps

13.† forget
filled
fixed

14. hop
shop
shot

15. dish
fish
figs

16. song
sock
long

17. hang
bags
bang

18. shell
shack
back

19.* who
was
went

20. fish
digs
dish

Use after page 24 of Unit 3. **Word Recognition:** See the inside back cover of the Teacher's Edition of this Skills Book for directions to administer the test.

*To test circle words

†To test applications of patterning

1.   The horse with the bell on its neck was locked in a little shed. It did not like the shed, so it kicked on the sills. The horse got mad.

Not Happy in the Shed

A Horse With a Bell

A Shed With Sills

2.   Dan will like his job. He will do things for Pam's dad, Mr. Benton, and his mom and dad. He will fix his bike with the cash he gets from them.

Mr. Benton and Dan

Dan's Job

The Red Bike

3.   Kim and Tam mixed figs and nuts in a pan and cooked them. Then they let Dot Bell have a mug of the jam. Dot licked her lips and said, "I like this jam very much."

Nut and Fig Jam

Dot's Pan

A Pan for Kim and Tam

Use after page 30 of Unit 4. **Main Idea:** Have pupils read the first paragraph. Then have them read the three titles below the paragraph and decide which one tells the main idea of the paragraph. Have them circle the correct title. Repeat for the remaining paragraphs having pupils work independently.

17

shop   wing   ring   shell   lock   mop

Use after page 30 of Unit 4. **Multiple Meanings:** Have pupils select a word from the top of the page that matches the first picture. Have them write the word on the line below the picture. Repeat for the remaining pictures having pupils work independently. Each of the words at the top of the page will be used two times on the page.

18

1. _____ shed was very hot.

   Grandma   Grandma's

2. We went with _____ to look for books.

   Grandpa   Grandpa's

3. "Let's pack _____ bags for her," said Dan.

   Jan   Jan's

4. The trip with _____ in his van went well.

   Gus   Gus's

5. The yams _____ cooks are good!

   Dad   Dad's

6. That _____ legs are very long.

   horse   horse's

Use after page 30 of Unit 4. **Possessive Forms:** Have pupils read the first sentence and decide which of the two words below it makes sense in the sentence. Have pupils circle the correct word and write it in the sentence. Repeat for the remaining sentences having pupils work independently.

19

1. If Tam gets her bike, _____

   _____.

2. If the kids go into the woods, _____

   _____.

3. If Dan and Jan don't get back to the house, _____

   _____.

4. If Jim, Kim, and Tam like chicken, _____

   _____.

she can run it on the path

they can have lunch with Jan and Dan

they can look at lots of things

they will not get the chicken wings

Use after page 30 of Unit 4. **Cause and Effect:** Pupils should carefully read the stories in Unit 4 before doing this exercise. Then have pupils read the first phrase and decide which of the phrases at the bottom of the page is a result of the first phrase. Have pupils write the most accurate phrase in the first sentence and cross out the phrase from the choice of phrases below. Repeat for the remaining phrases having pupils work independently.

1. The van hit a bad spot _____!

2. To look in a shop _____.

3. Nat is a cat, but _____.

4. You will like _____.

5. Ducks and hens _____.

Rags is a dog

and went bang

to sing good songs

have wings

is lots of fun

Use after page 30 of Unit 4. **Phrase Comprehension:** Have pupils read the first sentence. Then have them read the phrases at the bottom of the page and decide which phrase makes sense in the sentence. Have them write the correct phrase in the sentence and cross out the phrase from the choice of phrases below. Repeat for the remaining sentences having pupils work independently.

1. Pam <u>did</u> <u>not</u> have her bike.

   _____

2. Tam said that Ms. <u>Cook</u> <u>is</u> ill.

   _____

3. <u>I</u> <u>am</u> to go along with Mr. Benton.

   _____

4. "<u>Do</u> <u>not</u> miss the bus," said Dad.

   _____

5. <u>He</u> <u>is</u> very big for a pup.

   _____

6. The figs in this pan <u>are</u> <u>not</u> hot yet.

   _____

aren't   didn't   I'm   don't   he's   Cook's

Use after page 36 of Unit 5. **Contractions:** Have pupils read the first sentence and decide which contraction at the bottom of the page could be substituted for the underlined words in the sentence. Have them rewrite the sentence on the line provided, using the correct contraction. Have pupils cross out the contraction at the bottom of the page as they use them. Repeat for the remaining sentences having pupils work independently.

22

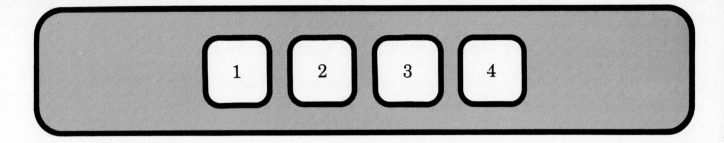

☐ Jim and Kim ran to school with Jan and Dan.

☐ The kids went into school as the bell rang.

1 Jan and Dan said good-by to Mom and Dad.

☐ Pam ran up to Jan, Dan, Kim, and Jim.

Use after page 36 of Unit 5. **Arranging Events in Sequence:** Pupils should carefully read the story on page 33 before doing this exercise. Then have pupils read all of the sentences on this page. Have them find the number **1** and read the sentence that tells what happened first. Then have them decide which event happened next and write the number **2** in the correct box. Repeat for the remaining sentences having pupils work independently. Pupils may copy the sentences in correct sequence on a separate sheet of paper.

23

1.   Pam said, "I like your mashed yams a lot, Mr. Bell."

Mr. Bell said, "Will you have lunch with us, then?"

_____

Pam said, "Yes, I will."   Pam said, "The figs are good."

2.   Tam had to have a tablet and pens for school.

But her mom didn't have the cash for them.

_____

She let Tam have a check.   Tam took wood chips to school.

3.   Tam's book bag has a rip in it.

Ms. Cook will fix it.

_____

Ms. Cook digs a ditch.   Tam will fill the bag with books.

4.   Jim and Kim like to sing very much.

So Ms. Cook let them sing for her room.

_____

They sang a long song.   They hid in the school.

Use after page 36 of Unit 5. **Making Inferences to Predict Outcomes:** Have pupils read the first two sentences at the top of the page. Then have them decide which of the two sentences below the line tells what might happen next. Have pupils circle the correct sentence and write it on the line. Repeat for the remaining sentences having pupils work independently.

24

1. Did the bell _____ yet?

    ring   hang   back

2. Jan is in _____ Cook's room at school.

    Gus   Ms.   Jim

3. At _____ we have lots of books.

    room   school   house

4. Dan has his _____ in his room.

    things   chins   bits

5. If the bell has _____, you run to school.

    picked   fed   rung

6. I have a _____ at school.

    van   shack   tablet

Use after page 36 of Unit 5. **Sentence Comprehension:** Have pupils read the first sentence and decide which of the three words below it makes sense in the sentence. Have them circle the correct word and write it in the sentence. Repeat for the remaining sentences having pupils work independently.

1. Ms. Cook's room was a good room.

   _____?

2. The bike will be fixed.

   _____?

3. A check is as good as cash.

   _____?

4. Rags was happy to be in school.

   _____?

5. Kim and Jim will have lunch with the Bells.

   _____?

6. You will like to fix the mashed yams.

   _____?

Use after page 36 of Unit 5. **Interrogative Transformations:** Have pupils read the first sentence. Then have them rearrange the words so that the sentence is asking something rather than telling something. Have pupils write the rearranged words on the line provided. Repeat for the remaining sentences having pupils work independently.

26

1. Nat tags along with the kids.

   The school bell rings.

   Nat _____.

   locks the van

   is at a shop

   is in school

2. Jan got a rash in the woods.

   Dan mops Jan's room for her.

   Jan _____.

   is happy with Dan

   has a fig

   is mad at Dan

3. Jan said to Jim, "I like bikes."

   Jan has no bike, but she has a little cash.

   Jan gets _____.

   a bus

   a dish

   a bike

Use after page 42 of Unit 6. **Making Inferences to Draw Conclusions:** Have pupils read the first two sentences and decide which of the three phrases below them makes sense in the third sentence. Have them circle the correct phrase and write it in the third sentence. Repeat for the remaining sentences having pupils work independently.

1. When the lunch bell rang, Ms. Cook's room was a mess. The cups and ripped lunch bags had to be picked up. Then the room had to be mopped.

Ripped Lunch Bags

The Mess in Ms. Cook's Room

The School Bell

2. Rags went to school to be with Dan, but she begged in the lunchroom. Dan yelled at her, but Rags looked at him and licked him. Dan was mad at Rags.

Dan at School

Rags Is a Bad Dog

Beg in the Kitchen

3. At Grandma's, Jan went to a dog shop with Dan. The little pups rubbed Jan's legs, and Jan missed Rags. She said, "I'll have a big hug for Rags when I see her."

Grandma and Grandpa's

The Little Pups

Rags Is Missed

Use after page 42 of Unit 6. **Main Idea:** Have pupils read the first paragraph. Then have them read the three titles below the paragraph and decide which one tells the main idea of the paragraph. Have them circle the correct title. Repeat for the remaining paragraphs having pupils work independently.

28

1. Dad _____ the kitchen when the kids were in school.

   mops   mopped

2. When Rags is good, Jan _____ her neck.

   rubs   rubbed

3. Kim had _____ the wood box with logs.

   fills   filled

4. Pam's chicken is _____ very well.

   cooks   cooked

5. Rags has _____ up the mess in the kitchen.

   licks   licked

6. Gus tells Pam a story and _____ her into bed.

   tucks   tucked

Use after page 42 of Unit 6. **Inflectional Endings -s, -ed:** Have pupils read the first sentence and decide which of the two words below it makes sense in the sentence. Have pupils circle the correct word and write it in the sentence. Repeat for the remaining sentences having pupils work independently.

29

Pam's Things To Do

✔ 1.   Go to the Benton Shop.

  ✔ a.   1 tablet

  ✔ b.   3 pens

     c.   1 bag of catnip

✔ 2.   Pick up things at the van shop.

  ✔ a.   1 latch

     b.   1 map

  ✔ c.   1 patch kit

1.   Was the tablet at the Benton Shop?   _____

2.   Did Pam get the map for the van?   _____

3.   Did Pam get the patch kit at the Benton Shop?   _____

4.   Did Pam get 3 pens?   _____

5.   Did Pam get the map and catnip?   _____

Use after page 42 of Unit 6. **Using a List:** Have pupils look at the list at the top of the page. Discuss with them the meaning of the list. Then have pupils read the first question at the bottom of the page. Have them answer the question with a *yes* or *no* on the line provided. Repeat for the remaining questions having pupils work independently.

30

When Rags is locked in the kitchen

If Jan locks Rags in the kitchen

If Rags sits up and begs

When Rags cannot see Dan and Jan at the house

1. _____

_____, she looks for them at school.

2. _____

_____, she will get bits of chicken from the boy.

3. _____

_____, she is not happy.

4. _____

_____, Jan will not have to miss lunch.

Use after page 42 of Unit 6. **Cause and Effect:** Pupils should carefully read the story beginning on page 38 before doing this exercise. Then have pupils read the first phrase and decide which of the numbered phrases at the bottom of the page is a result of the first phrase. Have pupils write the most accurate phrase in the correct sentence. Repeat for the remaining phrases having pupils work independently.

1.	2.	3.	4.
rips	cash	ring	runs
rubbed	hash	sick	rung
ripped	has	sing	hung

5.	6.†	7.	8.
wing	things	have	ripped
ring	wings	hang	rocks
rips	rings	rang	rubbed

9.	10.	11.	12.*
begged	shot	hung	bike
bucked	shop	hugs	little
mopped	ship	rung	like

13.†	14.	15.	16.
bench	wing	math	mopped
begin	thing	cash	missed
baths	with	mash	rubbed

17.	18.*	19.	20.
kicked	when	shed	thick
king	were	well	king
wing	who	shell	thing

Use after page 42 of Unit 6. **Word Recognition**: See the inside back cover of the Teacher's Edition of this Skills Book for directions to administer the test.

*To test circle words

†To test applications of patterning

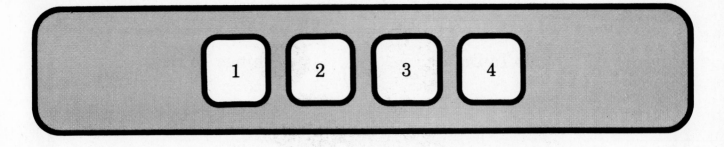

☐ Ms. Cook said, "Kim and Jim can sing that song well."

☐ Kim and Jim sang the song for Ms. King and Ms. Cook.

1 Ms. Cook went by Ms. King's room.

☐ Ms. King was humming and tapping a song.

Use after page 48 of Unit 7. **Arranging Events in Sequence:** Pupils should carefully read the story beginning on page 44 before doing this exercise. Then have pupils read all of the sentences on this page. Have them find the number **1** and read the sentence that tells what happened first. Then have them decide which event happened next and write the number **2** in correct box. Repeat for the remaining sentences having pupils work independently. Pupils may copy the sentences in correct sequence on a separate sheet of paper.

Things To Do	Things To Be In
_____	_____
_____	_____
_____	_____
_____	_____
_____	_____
_____	_____

a kitchen   tell a story

fix lunch   a bed

catch a bug   sing a song

a woodshed   a bus

pet a kitten   the bathroom

Use after page 48 of Unit 7. **Classification:** Have pupils find the words at the bottom of the page that make sense in the first column. Have them write the words on the lines in the first column and cross them out at the bottom of the page as they use them. Repeat for the remaining column having pupils work independently. Each group of words will be used only once.

1. "Sam, are you fixing your cab?" said Tam.

2. Ms. Cook said, "Who is humming that song?"

3. "Yes," said Jim, "I do like to sing."

4. "Rags! Rags!" yelled Jan, "Get the little box!"

5. "Rags is looking at the kitten," said Dan.

6. Kim said, "My books are missing!"

7. "Don't be mad," said Jim, "I have your books."

8. "When will we go to the shop?" said Mom.

9. Dad said, "I like sitting in the van with the kids."

10. "Jan," said Dan, "are you looking for Nat?"

Use after page 48 of Unit 7. **Punctuation:** Have pupils read the first sentence and draw a line under the speaker's exact words. Repeat for the remaining sentences having pupils work independently.

1. You can sing when you are _____ up.

2. I can see bikes _____ by my house.

3. Gus was _____ his woodshed.

4. Jim's tablet is _____ from his room.

5. Six chicks were _____ at the wood box.

6. Dad was _____ chicken in the kitchen.

7. Tam was happy as she did the job, _____ a song.

8. Sam was _____ in the cab of his van.

missing   fixing   sitting

tapping   passing   humming

Use after page 48 of Unit 7. **Sentence Comprehension:** Have pupils read the first sentence and find a word at the bottom of the page that makes sense in the sentence. Have pupils write the word in the sentence. Explain that a word may fit more than one sentence. Repeat for the remaining sentences having pupils work independently. Answers may vary.

36

1. Have you _____ your bags yet?

   packed   packs

2. When Nat _____ like that, he is not happy.

   looked   looks

3. Tam has _____ six rocks into the ditch.

   kicked   kicks

4. Ms. Long sees that the school is _____.

   locked   locks

5. Rags was bad and _____ up Dan's tablet.

   ripped   rips

6. Mr. Mills _____ songs that are happy.

   picked   picks

Use after page 48 of Unit 7. **Inflectional Endings -s, -ed:** Have pupils read the first sentence and decide which of the two words below it makes sense in the sentence. Have pupils circle the correct word and write it in the sentence. Repeat for the remaining sentences having pupils work independently.

1. Jim's bike had to be _____ when it had a bad spot.

   pitched   fixed   rubbed

2. Jim will _____ the fender.

   hit   wet   mend

3. Jim is going to lend his bike to _____.

   Kim   Pam   Tam

4. Pam gets a little _____ from a shop by her house.

   wood   tin   kit

5. Jim said that his bike will go like the _____ when it is fixed.

   hills   hogs   wind

6. Pam was _____ when Jim let her have his bike.

   sad   mad   happy

Use after page 54 of Unit 8. **Recalling Details:** Pupils should carefully read the story beginning on page 50 before doing this exercise. Then have the pupils read the first sentence and decide which of the words following the sentence is the most accurate. Have pupils circle the correct answer and write the words in the sentence. Repeat for the remaining sentences having pupils work independently.

38

1. Grandpa was humming in the kitchen and fixing lunch.

   But he forgot the hot pot.

   _____

   Grandpa had to mop up a mess.   The lunch was good.

2. Mrs. Bell went to get gas.

   She filled the van up.

   _____

   Mrs. Bell got a cab.   Mrs. Bell went on a trip.

3. "The bell is going to ring!" said Kim.

   "Let's go, then!" yelled Jim.

   _____

   Jim and Kim ran to school.   Jim and Kim sang songs.

4. Rags liked a funny little kitten.

   The kitten fell into a spot of mud.

   _____

   Rags licked the kitten.   Rags ran to the house.

Use after page 54 of Unit 8. **Making Inferences to Predict Outcomes:** Have pupils read the first two sentences at the top of the page. Then have them decide which of the two sentences below the line tells what might happen next. Have pupils circle the correct sentence and write it on the line. Repeat for the remaining sentences having pupils work independently.

39

1. When you are in school _____.

2. A bike fender of wood _____.

3. Tam and Dan ran _____.

4. You can lend your bike _____.

5. A dog is not happy _____.

you will sing songs

if you fix it

locked in the kitchen

will not bend much

to Mrs. Benton's shop

Use after page 54 of Unit 8. **Phrase Comprehension:** Have pupils read the first sentence. Then have them read the phrases at the bottom of the page and decide which phrase makes sense in the sentence. Have them write the correct phrase in the sentence and cross out the phrase from the choice of phrases below. Repeat for the remaining sentences having pupils work independently.

40

bend   punch   trip   rung   fish   passing

_____   _____   _____

_____   _____   _____

_____   _____   _____

_____   _____   _____

Use after page 54 of Unit 8. **Multiple Meanings:** Have pupils select a word from the top of the page that matches the first picture. Have them write the word on the line below the picture. Repeat for the remaining pictures having pupils work independently. Each of the words at the top of the page will be used two times on the page.

41

Jim has to bend the tin

When the bike is fixed

If Jim will lend the bike to Pam

Jim can't lend the bike to Pam

1. _____

_____, if it is not fixed.

2. _____

_____, it will go like the wind.

3. _____

_____, to get the bike fixed.

4. _____

_____, she will be good to it.

Use after page 54 of Unit 8. **Cause and Effect:** Pupils should carefully read the story beginning on page 50 before doing this exercise. Then have pupils read the first phrase and decide which of the numbered phrases at the bottom of the page could be a result of the first phrase. Have pupils write the first phrase in the correct sentence. Repeat for the remaining phrases having pupils work independently.

1. Gus and Pam like to go on trips in the van.

    But the van will not go.

    They _____.

    sing a funny song

    have to get gas

    mash yams in the van

2. When they got gas, Gus and Pam went fishing.

    Pam took hooks and a rod with her.

    She _____.

    picked a good spot by the pond to fish

    fixed bad spots in the fender

    pitched logs from the path

3. At the pond, Gus and Pam like to do little things.

    They like to sit in the sand by the pond.

    They _____.

    are filled with lunch

    have to go back on the sixth

    are fond of this pond

Use after page 60 of Unit 9. **Making Inferences to Draw Conclusions:** Have pupils read the first two sentences and decide which of the three phrases below them makes sense in the third sentence. Have them circle the correct phrase and write it in the third sentence. Repeat for the remaining sentences having pupils work independently.

1. cannot   _____   end

2. happy   _____   aren't

3. are   _____   can

4. begin   _____   sad

5. fat   _____   bad

6. did   _____   didn't

7. little   _____   thin

8. good   _____   big

Use after page 60 of Unit 9. **Antonyms:** Have pupils read the first word. Then have them decide which of the words on the right means the opposite of the first word. Have pupils write the correct word on the line after the first word and cross it out from the column on the right. Repeat for the remaining words having pupils work independently. Pupils may use the words to write original sentences.

1. Will we see a _____ with fish in it?

2. The fish is _____ of bugs in its pond.

3. Jim's job is to _____ things to Ms. Long.

4. Mom and Dad are _____ of Jan and Dan.

5. Jan said, "Will you _____ me a pen to go with my tablet, Pam?"

6. Check to see if _____ is in the box.

7. Kim will be in the _____ at school.

8. "I hang my jacket on a _____ at school," Pam said.

band   hand   pond

sand   fond   hook

Use after page 60 of Unit 9. **Sentence Comprehension:** Have pupils read the first sentence and find a word at the bottom of the page that makes sense in the sentence. Have pupils write the word in the sentence. Explain that a word may fit more than one sentence. Repeat for the remaining sentences having pupils work independently. Answers may vary.

1. It's fun to be in Ms. _____ room.

   King's   King

2. You can see the sky well at _____ house.

   Will's   Will

3. The _____ is in the kitchen at school.

   cook's   cook

4. The _____ is happy in this big pond.

   duck's   duck

5. Mrs. _____ shop is filled with good things.

   Benton's   Benton

6. Did the _____ dig and then run?

   dog's   dog

Use after page 60 of Unit 9. **Possessive Forms:** Have pupils read the first sentence and decide which of the two words below it makes sense in the sentence. Have pupils circle the correct word and write it in the sentence. Repeat for the remaining sentences having pupils work independently.

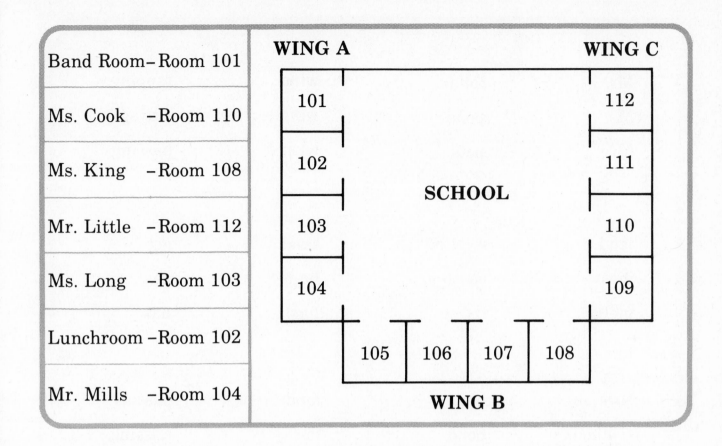

Band Room–Room 101

Ms. Cook   –Room 110

Ms. King   –Room 108

Mr. Little –Room 112

Ms. Long   –Room 103

Lunchroom –Room 102

Mr. Mills   –Room 104

WING A   **WING C**

101   112

102   111

SCHOOL

103   110

104   109

105 106 107 108

WING B

1.   Is Mr. Mills's room in Wing A?   _____

2.   When you go to room 101 from room 103, will you pass Mr.
      Little's room?   _____

3.   Is Mr. Little's room by the lunchroom?   _____

4.   Is Wing C by Wing A?   _____

5.   You have to go from Ms. Cook's room to the lunchroom.
      Do you go into Wing B to get to the lunchroom?   _____

Use after page 60 of Unit 9. **Using a Diagram:** Have pupils look at the diagram at the top of the page. Discuss with them the meaning of the diagram. Then have pupils read the first question at the bottom of the page. Have them answer the question with a *yes* or *no* on the line provided. Repeat for the remaining questions having pupils work independently.

47

1.*
Mr.
Ms.
Mrs.

2.
fond
pond
pots

3.
wind
wing
wish

4.
tapping
sitting
passing

5.
lend
mess
mend

6.
missing
passing
fixing

7.
sand
hand
hash

8.†
got
gas
has

9.†
sunfish
fishhook
sandbox

10.
bed
bend
mend

11.
fond
for
pond

12.
passing
missing
sitting

13.
sand
sang
hand

14.
send
end
lend

15.
fixing
looking
passing

16.
humming
sitting
tapping

17.*
spot
school
story

18.
passing
humming
looking

19.
bang
sand
band

20.
sand
send
bend

Use after page 60 of Unit 9. **Word Recognition:** See the inside back cover of the Teacher's Edition of this Skills Book for directions to administer the test.

48

*To test circle words

†To test applications of patterning

1.   Jim's pants were ripped, so he was going to mend them. He ran his hand on the legs of the pants, then took pins to fix the bad spot. The pants then fit well.

    Jim can mend his pants.

    Jim had pins.

    The pants legs were ripped.

2.   Six kids had songs to sing for the school band, but they forgot them. So Ms. Cook sang the songs with them. They liked Ms. Cook for that.

    Six kids sang for the school band.

    Ms. Cook can help.

    The kids forgot the songs.

3.   Pam set up a little tent by the pond. She hunted for bugs in the sand and fed the ducks. She picked up wood chips to send to Gus. And she went for dips in the pond. She was happy.

    Pam looked for bugs.

    Pam had fun at the pond.

    Pam went to get wood chips.

Use after page 66 of Unit 10. **Main Idea:** Have pupils read the first paragraph. Then have them read the three sentences below the paragraph and decide which one tells the main idea of the paragraph. Have them circle the correct sentence. Repeat for the remaining paragraphs having pupils work independently.

49

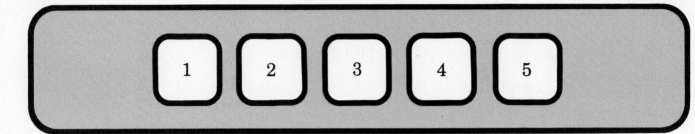

☐ Jan said to Dan, "Look in your tan pants."

☐ Dan looked in the kitchen and in his bedroom.

☐ Then Dan got a pen from a kit in the kitchen.

☐ Dan and Jan ran to the school bus with good pens.

1 Dan had things to get, and the school bus was passing by.

Use after page 66 of Unit 10. **Arranging Events in Sequence:** Pupils should carefully read the story beginning on page 62 before doing this exercise. Then have pupils read all of the sentences on this page. Have
them find the number **1** and read the sentence that tells what happened first. Then have them decide
which event happened next and write the number **2** in the correct box. Repeat for the remaining sentences
having pupils work independently. Pupils may copy the sentences in correct sequence on a separate sheet
of paper.

50

Good Things To Do:

1. _____

2. _____

3. _____

Bad Things To Do:

1. _____

2. _____

3. _____

Funny Things To Do:

1. _____

2. _____

3. _____

pitch a tent on a pond

cook lunch for Grandma and Grandpa

miss the school bus

get a cut on your hand

have a wood ship for lunch

mend the rip in your pants

mop the lunchroom

have a cat in a hat

get mud in your bed

Use after page 66 of Unit 10. **Classification:** Have pupils find the choices at the bottom of the page that belong under the first heading. Have them write the choices on the lines provided and cross them out at the bottom of the page as they use them. Repeat for the remaining headings having pupils work independently. Answers may vary.

51

1. "He is a good dad," said Jan.

    Jan   Tom   Tam

2. "We are going on a trip," said Gus and Pam.

    Nat and Rags   Gus and Jim   Pam and Gus

3. "Who is your mom, Kim?" said Gus.

    Tam's   Kim's   Gus's

4. "This is a very fat cat," said Grandpa.

    Nat   Grandpa   Dad

5. "I am fond of the sand at the pond," said Mom.

    Mrs. Benton   Mr. Mills   Sam

Use after page 66 of Unit 10. **Pronoun Referents:** Have pupils read the first sentence and decide which of the three choices below it means the same as the underlined word. Have pupils circle the correct words. Repeat for the remaining sentences having pupils work independently.

52

1. The kids will have to run for the school bus.

   _____?

2. We can hunt for Tam at Ben's ranch.

   _____?

3. They did catch a fish at the pond.

   _____?

4. Jim is fond of the school band.

   _____?

5. Pam will hop on the bike when it is fixed.

   _____?

6. Nat is going to look for bugs in the tent.

   _____?

Use after page 66 of Unit 10. **Interrogative Transformations:** Have pupils read the first sentence. Then have them rearrange the words so that the sentence is asking something rather than telling something. Have pupils write the rearranged words on the line provided. Repeat for the remaining sentences having pupils work independently.

1. Pam was going along the path on her bike.

    Then she got a chill.

    She said, "_____."

    I can see the sky

    I'll get wood chips for Dad

    I have to get my jacket

2. Ms. Cook was ill and was not at school.

    The kids cooked things and took them to her.

    Ms. Cook _____.

    was happy and got well

    was mad and yelled at the kids

    hung the things up on hooks

3. Dan took a nap in a tent.

    Jan hunted for wood chips and bugs.

    Dan and Jan were _____.

    at school

    in Ms. King's room

    in the woods

Use after page 66 of Unit 10. **Making Inferences to Draw Conclusions:** Have pupils read the first two sentences and decide which of the three phrases below them makes sense in the third sentence. Have them circle the correct phrase and write it in the third sentence. Repeat for the remaining sentences having pupils work independently.

54

1. no   _____   me

2. thin   _____   sick

3. you   _____   him

4. end   _____   can't

5. well   _____   yes

6. her   _____   don't

7. can   _____   thick

8. do   _____   begin

Use after page 66 of Unit 10. **Antonyms:** Have pupils read the first word. Then have them decide which of the words on the right means the opposite of the first word. Have pupils write the correct word on the line after the first word and cross it out from the column on the right. Repeat for the remaining words having pupils work independently. Pupils may use the words to write original sentences.

55

1. Mr. and Mrs. Benton are going to get bunk beds. □

2. The bunk beds will be for Jim's room. □

3. Mr. Benton sees a big fish tank in the bank. □

4. The pet shop has no tank, so they look in a junk shop. □

5. Jim will get the tank for his cat. □

6. Six shells sank onto the sand. □

7. Kim and Jim like the fish and thank Mr. Benton. □

8. Mrs. Benton rubs her hand as she gets back from the bank. □

Use after page 72 of Unit 11. **Recalling Details:** Pupils should carefully read the story beginning on page 68 before doing this exercise. Then have pupils read the first sentence and decide whether it is true or false. If it is true, have them put an **X** in the box. Repeat for the remaining sentences having pupils work independently.

56

1. <u>We</u> <u>are</u> looking for a map.

   _____

2. "<u>I</u> <u>will</u> look in here," said Dad.

   _____

3. This <u>dog</u> <u>is</u> going fishing with Kim.

   _____

4. "<u>You</u> <u>will</u> like this book," said Ms. Cook.

   _____

5. Kim <u>Benton</u> <u>is</u> in this room.

   _____

6. "<u>I</u> <u>have</u> got to get the kids!" Dad said.

   _____

I've   dog's   we're   I'll   Benton's   you'll

Use after page 72 of Unit 11. **Contractions:** Have pupils read the first sentence and decide which contraction at the bottom of the page could be substituted for the underlined words in the sentence. Have them rewrite the sentence on the line provided, using the correct contraction. Have pupils cross out the contraction at the bottom of the page as they use them. Repeat for the remaining sentences having pupils work independently.

1. Tam hopped onto the fender of the van.

 The van began to go.

 _____

 Tam fell and rubbed her leg.   Tam hunted for bugs.

2. Pam liked to go to the pond.

 She sat on the bank of the pond.

 _____

 She looked at the fish.   Pam missed her cat.

3. The bugs are thick at the pond.

 Tam has a net.

 _____

 Tam will catch the bugs.   Tam will thank the bugs.

4. Dan and Jan began school.

 Rags missed them.

 _____

 So Rags sat in the sink.   So Rags went to school.

Use after page 72 of Unit 11. **Making Inferences to Predict Outcomes:** Have pupils read the first two sentences at the top of the page. Then have them decide which of the two sentences below the line tells what might happen next. Have pupils circle the correct sentence and write it on the line. Repeat for the remaining sentences having pupils work independently.

1. The little shop had _____ as well as good things.

2. A _____ has cash for your check.

3. The sand and shells _____ in the tank.

4. Kim said, "_____ you for the fish, Dad."

5. Do you _____ a fish will sink?

6. The _____ ink is from a red pen.

7. The little ship had a bad spot, so it _____.

8. Can you see the _____ fish?

thank   think   junk

pink   bank   sank

Use after page 72 of Unit 11. **Sentence Comprehension:** Have pupils read the first sentence and find a word at the bottom of the page that makes sense in the sentence. Have pupils write the word in the sentence. Explain that a word may fit more than one sentence. Repeat for the remaining sentences having pupils work independently. Answers may vary

1.   Jim is _____ his bike in the shed.

         fixed   fixing

2.   Mrs. Benton _____ her hand when she got to the shop.

         rubbed   rubbing

3.   _____ at the sky is fun.

         Looked   Looking

4.   Jan got cash for _____ Grandpa's van.

         fixed   fixing

5.   The bus we were on _____ Sid's ranch.

         passed   passing

6.   Ms. Long _____ as she filled the sandbox.

         hummed   humming

Use after page 72 of Unit 11. **Inflectional Endings -ed, -ing:** Have pupils read the first sentence and decide which of the two words below it makes sense in the sentence. Have pupils circle the correct word and write it in the sentence. Repeat for the remaining sentences having pupils work independently.

60

1. _____ fender

2. _____ kitten

3. _____ fog

4. _____ house

5. _____ nuts

6. _____ rods

the hot mixed

the thick wet

a bent tin

a funny little

the long thin

the big wood

Use after page 72 of Unit 11. **Adjectives:** Have pupils read the first word at the top of the page. Then have them decide which group of adjectives at the bottom of the page describes the first word. Have pupils write the correct group of adjectives on the line in front of the first word. Have them cross out each group of adjectives at the bottom of the page as they use it. Repeat for the remaining words having pupils work independently. Each group of adjectives will be used only once. Answers may vary. Accept all reasonable answers.

61

1. Cooks fix chicken _____.

   in the kitchen

   can fish

   going for chicken

2. The pen at the bank _____.

   to cash a check

   got ink on Gus's pants

   for Mrs. Benton

3. Six bedrooms are _____.

   from the woods

   a big sack of chicken

   in the house

Use after page 72 of Unit 11. **Phrase Comprehension:** Have pupils read the first sentence and decide which of the three phrases below it makes sense in the sentence. Have them circle the correct phrase and write it in the sentence. Repeat for the remaining sentences having pupils work independently.

62

1.
hut
hunt
hum

2.*
room
from
rock

3.
ink
think
sink

4.
lent
dent
bent

5.
bank
band
sank

6.
sent
bent
send

7.†
into
onto
on

8.
pan
pants
paths

9.
think
pin
pink

10.
bunch
junk
bunk

11.
thank
think
sank

12.*
her
were
here

13.
sand
sank
tank

14.
tent
dent
ten

15.
sip
sink
pink

16.†
I'll
I'm
I've

17.
bent
dent
den

18.
tank
tan
bank

19.
bunk
junk
jug

20.
sink
think
thank

Use after page 72 of Unit 11. **Word Recognition:** See the inside back cover of the Teacher's Edition of this Skills Book for directions to administer the test.

*To test circle words

†To test applications of patterning

63

1. Pam has dusted her bedroom.

_____?

2. This isn't Ms. Cook's or Ms. King's room.

_____?

3. Gus wasn't selling his van.

_____?

4. Dinner is better than lunch here.

_____?

5. The sun is sinking past the woods.

_____?

6. You must have lists when you shop.

_____?

Use after page 78 of Unit 12. **Interrogative Transformations:** Have pupils read the first sentence. Then have them rearrange the words so that the sentence is asking something rather than telling something. Have pupils write the rearranged words on the line provided. Repeat for the remaining sentences having pupils work independently.

64

1. Dan mopped his bedroom and the bathroom.

   He mixed Nat's lunch and fed him.

   Mr. Bell said, "_____."

   You can't have lunch, Dan

   You have to have a bath, Dan

   You did very well, Dan

2. Mr. Sands packs his bag to go on a trip.

   But he gets a bad rash.

   Mr. Sands cannot _____.

   cook yams for Pam

   go on the trip

   look for ducks

3. Gus's yams were on top in the pot.

   But then he did not see them.

   As they cooked, the yams _____.

   sank in the pot

   fell into the dust

   got mashed up

Use after page 78 of Unit 12. **Making Inferences to Draw Conclusions:** Have pupils read the first two sentences and decide which of the three phrases below them makes sense in the third sentence. Have them circle the correct phrase and write it in the third sentence. Repeat for the remaining sentences having pupils work independently.

1. they   we   us   them   you   sandbox

2. shell   fish   tank   think   ship   rod

3. doctor   Jan   Kim   Jim   Dan   Tam

4. horse   fox   kitten   tablet   duck   chicken

5. leg   fist   ditch   back   chin   neck

6. bank   house   shed   shack   school   fog

7. licked   hum   said   begged   yelled   sang

8. dish   pan   mug   pot   cup   rug

Use after page 78 of Unit 12. **Classification:** Have pupils look at the first row of words and decide which word does not belong in the row. Have them draw a line through that word. Repeat for the remaining rows of words having pupils work independently. Pupils' answers may vary within reason.

1. last at bell the rang

   _____.

2. your dust bedroom must you

   _____.

3. list things the do to

   _____.

4. little it's a just dent

   _____.

5. fast very van the went

   _____.

6. went house we past her

   _____.

Use after page 78 of Unit 12. **Sentence Comprehension:** Have pupils read the first group of scrambled words. Then have them decide how the words could be rearranged to make a sentence. Have them write the sentence on the line provided. Repeat for the remaining groups of words having pupils work independently. Answers may vary.

1. If Gus and Pam have dinner with the Bells, _____

   _____ .

2. Mr. Bell cooks such good chicken, _____

   _____ .

3. If Gus and Pam aren't at the house by six, _____

   _____ .

4. When the bell rang, _____

   _____ .

so Jan got lots of it

Mr. Bell went to let Gus and Pam in

Mr. Bell will go to look for them

the Bells have lots to do

Use after page 78 of Unit 12. **Cause and Effect:** Pupils should carefully read the story beginning on page 74 before doing this exercise. Then have pupils read the first phrase and decide which of the phrases at the bottom of the page could be a result of the first phrase. Have pupils write the correct phrase in the first sentence and cross out the phrase from the choice of phrases below. Repeat for the remaining phrases having pupils work independently.

68

☐ At the shop Jim went up a ladder.

1 The Bentons' list had bunk beds on it.

☐ The Bentons shopped for the rest of the things and had fun.

☐ Then the Bentons looked at chests to match the beds.

☐ The shop had a van to get to the Bentons' house.

Use after page 84 of Unit 13. **Arranging Events in Sequence**: Pupils should carefully read the story begin-ning on page 82 before doing this exercise. Then have pupils read all of the sentences on this page. Have them find the number **1** and read the sentence that tells what happened first. Then have them decide which event happened next and write the number **2** in the correct box. Repeat for the remaining sentences having pupils work independently. Pupils may copy the sentences in correct sequence on a separate sheet of paper.

69

1. Jim was going to miss his dinner.

    "I must get home," he said.

    _____

    Jim went home fast.   Jim looked at a book.

2. Gus has six things he must do.

    So he will check his list.

    _____

    Then he will sell his vests.   Then he will not forget the things.

3. "We're going to Dan's house," said Tam and Jim.

    "So will I, then," said Pam.

    _____

    Pam has dinner.   Pam gets her bike.

4. Mrs. Benton was selling her van.

    Dot Bell liked the van very much.

    _____

    Dot Bell got the van.   Mrs. Benton looked for a van.

Use after page 84 of Unit 13. **Making Inferences to Predict Outcomes:** Have pupils read the first two sentences at the top of the page. Then have them decide which of the two sentences below the line tells what might happen next. Have pupils circle the correct sentence and write it on the line. Repeat for the remaining sentences having pupils work independently.

1. "My bike has a big dent in it!" said Pam.

2. "Can we mend the dent?" said Grandma.

3. "Is this pen filled with ink?" said Mrs. Benton.

4. A sunset in the hills is a good thing to see!

5. Rags shook dust on Jan and Dan's dinner!

6. "Are the eggs in this nest robin's eggs?" said Gus.

_____

_____

_____

Use after page 84 of Unit 13. **Punctuation:** Have pupils read the first sentence. If the sentence shows ex-citement, have them copy it in the space provided at the bottom of the page. Repeat for the remaining sentences having pupils work independently.

71

1. bus   _____   hat

2. cut   _____   shack

3. cap   _____   chop

4. sick   _____   spot

5. shed   _____   cot

6. bed   _____   bag

7. sack   _____   van

8. dot   _____   ill

Use after page 84 of Unit 13. **Synonyms:** Have pupils read the first word. Then have them decide which of the words on the right means almost the same as the first word. Have pupils write the correct word on the line after the first word and cross it out from the column on the right. Repeat for the remaining words having pupils work independently. Pupils may use the words to write original sentences.

72

1. "Dan is a boy <u>who</u> can sing well," said Gus.

      Dan   Jim   Gus

2. "You must dust <u>your</u> room, Jim," said Dad.

      Dad   Ms. Cook   Jim

3. Jim, Kim, and Mrs. Benton looked at the sinking sunset.
<u>They</u> liked it very much.

      The Bentons   Mrs. Benton   Jim and Kim

4. "I will sell <u>you</u> my fish, Pam," said Jim.

      Jan   Jim   Pam

5. Rags liked to get into junk.
So Dan locked <u>her</u> up.

      Rags   Dan   Jan

Use after page 84 of Unit 13. **Pronoun Referents:** Have pupils read the first sentence and decide which of the three choices below it means the same as the underlined word. Have pupils circle the correct words. Repeat for the remaining sentences having pupils work independently.

73

1. Dan must have six _____ for school.   (tablet)

2. _____ and girls like to go shopping.   (boy)

3. The _____ were on the pans.   (lid)

4. Jan sang _____ as she packed her bag.   (song)

5. I got eggs from six _____.   (chicken)

6. "The _____ are not bad," said Sid.   (dent)

7. Ten _____ were in Ms. Cook's room.   (girl)

8. Jim and Dan had _____ that looked like cats.   (mask)

9. Rags and Nat are Jan and Dan's _____.   (pet)

Use after page 90 of Unit 14. **Plurals:** Have pupils read the first sentence and notice the word in parentheses at the end of it. Then have them change the word in parentheses so that it means more than one and makes sense in the sentence. Have pupils write the word in the sentence. Repeat for the remaining sentences having pupils work independently.

1. Is the cut on _____ leg better?

   Pam   Pam's

2. This is _____ jam she got from the little boy.

   Mom   Mom's

3. Ben's _____ are the best.

   chickens   chicken's

4. The chips and buns are _____.

   Grandpa   Grandpa's

5. _____ pants, vest, and socks are very big on him.

   Jim   Jim's

6. _____ is not happy when the kids fuss with her.

   Rags   Rags's

Use after page 90 of Unit 14. **Possessive Forms:** Have pupils read the first sentence and decide which of the two words below it makes sense in the sentence. Have pupils circle the correct word and write it in the sentence. Repeat for the remaining sentences having pupils work independently.

1. the boy gum ask for

_____.

2. gift dog is a the

_____.

3. school my desk at is

_____.

4. the lifts girl the bunk

_____.

5. the funny is mask very

_____.

6. number disks fun are the

_____.

Use after page 90 of Unit 14. **Sentence Comprehension:** Have pupils read the first group of scrambled words. Then have them decide how the words could be rearranged to make a sentence. Have them write the sentence on the line provided. Repeat for the remaining groups of words having pupils work independently. Answers may vary.

76

1. "Dogs are the best _____," said Tam.

   pet   pets

2. "Is your _____ in the bag?" asked Jan.

   books   book

3. Jim got to his _____ last.

   desks   desk

4. "I'll have a little _____ of chicken," said Gus.

   bit   bits

5. The boys checked to see if the _____ were bent.

   bikes   bike

6. The kids looked at six _____ in a pen.

   pig   pigs

Use after page 90 of Unit 14. **Plurals:** Have the pupils read the first sentence and decide which of the word choices belongs in the blank. Have them circle the word and write it in the blank. Repeat for the remaining sentences having pupils work independently.

77

PAM'S MATH TESTS

BEST

BETTER

GOOD

BAD

Test 1   Test 2   Test 3   Test 4

1. Did Pam do best on Test 1?   _____

2. Is Test 3 the best test?   _____

3. Is Test 2 just as good as Test 4?   _____

4. Are Test 2 and Test 4 **BETTER** tests?   _____

5. Did Pam do better on Test 2 than on Test 1?___

Use after page 90 of Unit 14. **Using a Graph:** Have pupils look at the graph at the top of the page. Discuss with them the meaning of the graph. Then have pupils read the first question at the bottom of the page. Have them answer the question with a *yes* or *no* on the line provided. Repeat for the remaining questions having pupils work independently.

78

1.
desk
dent
disk

2.
fast
last
lap

3.
bend
pest
best

4.
fist
fish
list

5.
just
mud
must

6.
lip
lift
gift

7.*
good
got
girl

8.
fast
fat
past

9.
nest
tent
test

10.
dish
desk
disk

11.
mask
ask
mash

12.†
wooden
wood
woodshed

13.
fist
list
lick

14.
west
test
vest

15.
junk
just
dust

16.†
shop
hook
shook

17.
west
rest
red

18.*
horse
home
house

19.
gift
get
lift

20.
nest
chest
check

Use after page 90 of Unit 14. **Word Recognition:** See the inside back cover of the Teacher's Edition of this Skills Book for directions to administer the test.

*To test circle words

†To test applications of patterning

79

1. A robin's eggs fell from the nest.

   Dan asked Jim to help the robin.

   Jim _____.

         picked the eggs up and took them to the nest

         ran to play at Jan's house

         began to dig a ditch

2. Grandfather ripped his vest and had to mend it.

   He did a good job with it.

   He said, "_____."

         This vest fits like it did

         I'll go shopping for a vest

         I took a bath

3. Gus got Pam a desk as a gift.

   Pam said, "This is the best desk."

   Pam _____.

         liked her gift very much

         took the desk back to the shop

         got rid of the desk fast

Use after page 96 of Unit 15. **Making Inferences to Draw Conclusions:** Have pupils read the first two sentences and decide which of the three phrases below them makes sense in the third sentence. Have them circle the correct phrase and write it in the third sentence. Repeat for the remaining sentences having pupils work independently.

80

1. Little Bud _____ at bugs when he sees them.

   hits   hitting

2. Grandma is _____ Nat play next to the woodshed.

   lets   letting

3. Jim can go on a trip when he _____ his bike.

   checks   checking

4. That tapping was Ms. King _____ the bells.

   hits   hitting

5. As he dusted, Dan was _____ up things in his room.

   picks   picking

6. Mom _____ happy when she is fishing.

   looks   looking

Use after page 96 of Unit 15. **Inflectional Endings -s, -ing:** Have pupils read the first sentence and decide which of the two words below it makes sense in the sentence. Have pupils circle the correct word and write it in the sentence. Repeat for the remaining sentences having pupils work independently.

81

1. To help the cut, a pad is _____.

2. When the kids left school, _____.

3. Boys and girls have fun _____.

4. The little kitten held _____.

5. I get my socks and vest _____.

on my left hand

on the bus

from my room

they ran to play

onto Dan's lap

Use after page 96 of Unit 15. **Phrase Comprehension:** Have pupils read the first sentence. Then have them read the phrases at the bottom of the page and decide which phrase makes sense in the sentence. Have them write the correct phrase in the sentence and cross out the phrase from the choice of phrases below. Repeat for the remaining sentences having pupils work independently.

vest	dip	sell
_____	_____	_____
_____	_____	_____
_____	_____	_____
_____	_____	_____
_____	_____	_____

chest	ship	tell
zip	pest	sip
bell	fell	west
rest	best	rip
tip	shell	nest

Use after page 96 of Unit 15. **Classifying Words by Patterns:** Have pupils find the words at the bottom of the page that belong in the first column. Have them write the words on the lines in the first column and cross them out at the bottom of the page as they use them. Repeat for the remaining columns having pupils work independently. Each word will be used only once.

83

pot   tablets   sink   band   chest   bank

_____   _____   _____

_____   _____   _____

_____   _____   _____

_____   _____   _____

Use after page 96 of Unit 15. **Multiple Meanings:** Have pupils select a word from the top of the page that matches the first picture. Have them write the word on the line below the picture. Repeat for the remaining pictures having pupils work independently. Each of the words at the top of the page will be used two times on the page.

84

| 1 | Playing in her room, Pam made masks for a play at school. |

| | The school play was very funny with Pam's funny masks. |

| | The boys and girls looked like ducks and horses in the masks. |

| | Tam went to Pam's house to see the masks. |

| | Mr. Sands and Tam went to see Pam's play at school. |

Use after page 102 of Unit 16. **Arranging Events in Sequence:** Pupils should carefully read the story beginning on page 98 before doing this exercise. Then have pupils read all of the sentences on this page. Have them find the number **1** and read the sentence that tells what happened first. Then have them decide which event happened next and write the number **2** in the correct box. Repeat for the remaining sentences having pupils work independently. Pupils may copy the sentences in correct sequence on a separate sheet of paper.

85

When Chester hid from Pam

If Pam will let Chester be a dog

When Pam gets home from school

When Pam likes to play that Chester is a doll

1. _____

_____, Chester will run under her bed.

2. _____

_____, he gets mad.

3. _____

_____, she felt sad.

4. _____

_____, he will not run under her bed.

Use after page 102 of Unit 16. **Cause and Effect:** Pupils should carefully read the story beginning on page 100 before doing this exercise. Then have pupils read the first phrase and decide which of the numbered phrases at the bottom of the page could be a result of the first phrase. Have pupils write the first phrase in the correct sentence. Repeat for the remaining phrases having pupils work independently.

86

1. puppy bed the under hid

   The _____.

2. held Jan's Dad hand left

   Dad _____.

3. has he good silk a vest

   He _____.

4. he cup milk a had of

   He _____.

5. dog can't a be doll a

   A _____.

6. Jim box made wood from a

   Jim _____.

Use after page 102 of Unit 16. **Sentence Comprehension:** Have pupils read the first group of scrambled words. Then have them decide how the words could be rearranged to make a sentence. Point out to pupils that the first word of the sentence has been given to them. Have them write the remainder of the sentence on the line provided. Repeat for the remaining groups of words having pupils work independently. Answers may vary.

87

1. _____ fish

2. _____ fox

3. _____ bag

4. _____ bus

5. _____ wind

6. _____ bedroom

a passing school

the fast west

Jim's lunch

a wet pink

Pam's dusted

a red hunted

Use after page 102 of Unit 16. **Adjectives:** Have pupils read the first word at the top of the page. Then have them decide which group of adjectives at the bottom of the page describes the first word. Have pupils write the correct group of adjectives on the line in front of the first word. Have them cross out each group of adjectives at the bottom of the page as they use it.   Repeat for the remaining words having pupils work independently. Each group of adjectives will be used only once. Answers may vary. Accept all reasonable answers.

88

1. My _____ house is filled with little cups.

    doll's   dolls

2. That was the day Pam made _____ dinner.

    Chester's   Chester

3. We will mend the silk masks in Ms. _____ room.

    Cook's   Cook

4. The Bentons like _____ mashed yams.

    Sid's   Sid

5. _____ kitten and pup made her happy.

    Tam's   Tam

6. We had to hunt for the fishhook in _____ bag.

    Kim's   Kim

Use after page 102 of Unit 16. **Possessive Forms:** Have pupils read the first sentence and decide which of the two words below it makes sense in the sentence. Have pupils circle the correct word and write it in the sentence. Repeat for the remaining sentences having pupils work independently.

1. _____ can't go to school when he has a rash.

     Dan   Nat   Mr. Bell

2. Rags and Dan were sitting in the _____.

     tub   tent   van

3. Mrs. Bell has Dan sit next to the _____ so she can
   see him better.

     lamp   TV   bed

4. Dan felt better when Mrs. Bell got his _____.

     dinner   rash   lunch

5. When he was at home, Dan looked at his _____.

     math book   jacket   bike

6. Dan felt that his rash helped him with his _____.

     fishing   math   humming

Use after page 107 of Unit 17. **Recalling Details:** Pupils should carefully read the story beginning on page 104 before doing this exercise. Then have the pupils read the first sentence and decide which of the words following the sentence is the most accurate. Have pupils circle the correct answer and write the words in the sentence. Repeat for the remaining sentences having pupils work independently.

1. The girls and boys in Ms. Cook's room had a day to go to camp. They took milk, figs, and eggs. After lunch they sang songs sitting on the sand.

   Ms. Cook's room went to camp.

   The kids took figs and milk.

   They sang on the sand.

2. Tam jumped on the deck and got a cut. Dan got a bump on his leg from his bike. Pam had a rash. Kim had the mumps. And Jan felt ill and had to go to bed.

   Bikes are fun.

   The kids are not well.

   Jan went to bed.

3. Kim has a big red gas lamp in her room. She got it from her mom, who got it from her grandfather. It has dents in it, but Kim likes it to help her look at books.

   Kim has a gas lamp.

   The lamp has dents in it.

   The lamp was Mrs. Benton's.

Use after page 107 of Unit 17. **Main Idea:** Have pupils read the first paragraph. Then have them read the three sentences below the paragraph and decide which one tells the main idea of the paragraph. Have them circle the correct sentence. Repeat for the remaining paragraphs having pupils work independently.

1. My <u>doll</u> <u>is</u> going to like this jacket.

   _____

2. The robin eggs <u>are</u> <u>not</u> in here.

   _____

3. <u>Chester</u> <u>is</u> not happy with Pam.

   _____

4. Rags <u>was</u> <u>not</u> locked in the kitchen.

   _____

5. Maybe <u>we</u> <u>will</u> see a sunset.

   _____

6. The <u>chicken</u> <u>is</u> playing with Nat!

   _____

Chester's   we'll   doll's   chicken's   aren't   wasn't

Use after page 107 of Unit 17. **Contractions:** Have pupils read the first sentence and decide which contraction at the bottom of the page could be substituted for the underlined words in the sentence. Have them rewrite the sentence on the line provided, using the correct contraction. Have pupils cross out the contractions at the bottom of the page as they use them. Repeat for the remaining sentences having pupils work independently.

92

1. house   _____   tapping

2. hitting   _____   hen

3. mend   _____   home

4. chicken   _____   bucked

5. kicked   _____   fat

6. well   _____   fix

7. rubbed   _____   felt

8. thick   _____   good

Use after page 107 of Unit 17. **Synonyms:** Have pupils read the first word. Then have them decide which of the words on the right means almost the same as the first word. Have pupils write the correct word on the line after the first word and cross it out from the column on the right. Repeat for the remaining words having pupils work independently. Pupils may use the words to write original sentences.

93

1. Jim got big, and his bike was little.

   He had to have cash to get a bike that fit him.

   _____

   Jim shopped for a belt.   Jim had to sell his bike.

2. "Will you help me sell my bike, Mom?" Jim asked.

   Mrs. Benton said, "Yes, I will, but I can't help today."

   _____

   Jim ran away.   Mrs. Benton helped Jim the next day.

3. Dan's rash had little bumps.
   But they did not itch.

   _____

   Dan had milk for dinner.   The rash went away.

4. Tam lifted herself onto a wooden horse.
   She ripped her pants.

   _____

   Dad helped fix the rip.   Tam sang a song.

Use after page 107 of Unit 17. **Making Inferences to Predict Outcomes:** Have pupils read the first two sentences at the top of the page. Then have them decide which of the two sentences below the line tells what might happen next. Have pupils circle the correct sentence and write it on the line. Repeat for the remaining sentences having pupils work independently.

94

1.†
tent
rent
rush

2.
belt
felt
bell

3.
next
nest
neck

4.
must
mumps
bump

5.
milk
sink
silk

6.
last
camp
lamp

7.
left
let
luck

8.*
play
doll
day

9.
melt
mend
felt

10.
kept
kick
kiss

11.
silk
milk
mix

12.
jump
junk
lump

13.†
away
after
along

14.
held
hill
help

15.
lump
bump
luck

16.
help
held
hid

17.
bump
jump
bunk

18.
melt
felt
fell

19.
camp
cash
lamp

20.*
my
made
said

Use after page 107 of Unit 17. **Word Recognition:** See the inside back cover of the Teacher's Edition of this Skills Book for directions to administer the test.

*To test circle words

†To test applications of patterning

95

INDEX TO SKILLS

Phrase Comprehension—*1, 21, 40, 62, 82*

Recalling Details—*2, 13, 38, 56, 74, 90*

Pronoun Referents—*3, 12, 52, 73*

Punctuation—*4, 35, 71*

Cause and Effect—*5, 20, 31, 42, 68, 86*

Arranging Events in Sequence—*6, 23, 33, 50, 69, 85*

Contractions—*7, 22, 57, 92*

Interrogative Transformations—*8, 26, 53, 64*

Sentence Comprehension—*9, 25, 36, 45, 59, 67, 76, 87*

Main Idea—*10, 17, 28, 49, 77, 91*

Making Inferences to Draw Conclusions—*11, 27, 43, 54, 65, 80*

Classification—*14, 34, 51, 66, 83*

Adjectives—*15, 61, 88*

Word Recognition—*16, 32, 48, 63, 79, 95*

Multiple Meanings—*18, 41, 84*

Possessive Forms—*19, 46, 75, 89*

Making Inferences to Predict Outcomes—*24, 39, 58, 70, 94*

Inflectional Endings—*29, 37, 60, 81*

Everyday Living Skills—*30, 47, 78*

Antonyms—*44, 55*

Synonyms—*72, 93*

Plurals—*74, 77*

GET SET
Merrill Reading Program
Fifth Edition

1. fish
    dish
    fits

2. wing
    ring
    rung

3. bend
    mend
    bang

4. hung
    hang
    rang

5. dot
   don't
   didn't

6. who
   when
   west

7. room
   rush
   rim

8. we're
   went
   were

9. yes
   yams
   yours

10. bikes
    liked
    licked

11. her
    hens
    hers

12. chicken
    kitchen
    kitten

13. _____

14. _____

15. _____

16. _____

17.   Dan went to the shop to get a lot of things. He got a mug, six hooks, a ring, a tablet, and a jacket. Dan forgot to get cash from his Grandpa. He had to go back to his house to get the cash.

> Dan got a mug, six hooks, a ring, a tablet, and a jacket at the shop.
> Dan forgot to get the cash from his Grandpa.
> Dan got lots of things, but he had to go back to his house to get the cash.

18. Dan forgot _____.

> to go to the shop to get a ring
> to get the cash from his Grandpa
> the mug, the ring, and a tablet

19.   Jan can sing very, very well. She has a lot of songs she can sing. She will sing when she is on her bike. She will sing to her cat and its kittens. She will sing in the lunchroom, in the bedrooms, in the bathroom, and in the kitchen. Jan has a wish to sing her songs for a king.

Jan will sing to her cat and its kitten.

Jan has a wish to sing her songs for a king.

Jan can sing a lot of songs.

20.   Jan can sing to her _____.

cat and its kittens

king

songs

21.   Sam took a long trip on a big ship. This was his sixth trip on a ship. He was happy he didn't get sick on this trip. He had lots of things to do on the ship, but it was a very long trip and he missed Jan and Dan a lot. He packed shells into a box for Jan and Dan when he got back.

Sam had lots of things to do on his long trip on a ship.
Sam took a long trip and packed shells for Dan and Jan.
Sam didn't get sick on his sixth trip.

22. Sam packed _____.

fish

ship

shells

23.   Rags had a long nap in the shed at Grandma's house. When Rags got up, the latch on the shed was locked. Rags was not happy to be locked in the shed! She had to bang and bang on that woodshed. Pam was passing by the shed when Rags was locked in. She got Grandma to fix the lock and get Rags from the shed. Rags was so happy, she licked Pam's leg.

When Rags got up from her nap, the shed was locked.

Rags had to bang on the shed.

Rags was locked in, and Pam got Rags from the shed.

24.   Rags had to bang on _____.

the shed

the latch

the lock

25. Kim's   went   to   they   red   house

_____

26. her   Jan   lunch   rip   sack   did

_____

27. took   trip   the   bike   long   Dan

_____

28. for   looking   Gus   his   jacket   was

_____

shell   punch   shop   ring   pass   trip

29. _____ 30. _____ 31. _____

32. _____ 33. _____ 34. _____

35. _____ 36. _____ 37. _____

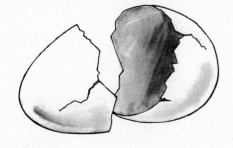  

38. _____ 39. _____ 40. _____

109

41.   Nat has a nap in the shed.

Grandpa locks the latch on the shed.

Nat _____.

can see the TV

cannot run to Jan

has bits of fish

42.   Jan is sick with a chill and a rash.

She cannot go to school.

Jan _____.

is on her bike on the path

will bat and run a lot

will have to have a pill

43. Jim and Kim like chicken for lunch.

    If Dad cooks lots of chicken, Jim and Kim

    _____.

    will have a good lunch

    cannot have fun

    have ham and buns

44. Dad and Dan are going to the pond.

    They have rods and hooks in a bag.

    They are going _____.

    hunting

    fishing

    jumping

45.   Grandma got her checkbook from the box in her kitchen. She got a cab that took her to the shop. At the shop she got chicken, buns, chips, and dip. Grandma was not happy that the shop had no ham for her.

Grandma then looked for a cab to go back to her house. She looked and looked but a cab did not pass by.

[ ]   A cab did not pass by.

[1]   Grandma got her checkbook.

[ ]   Grandma took a cab to the shop.

[ ]   She got chicken, buns, chips, and dip.

46.   Jim's dad took him to see the doctor. The doctor had to check Jim's rash. The doctor looked at the rash and said, "You did not rub the rash and it is well." Jim did not fuss so his dad got him a little ship at a shop. Then Jim went back to school.

[1]   Jim and his dad went to the doctor.

[ ]   Jim got a little ship.

[ ]   Jim went to school.

[ ]   The doctor checked Jim's rash.

47.   Gus looked at a kitten in the ditch. It was a very little kitten with no house. The kitten was wet and it had a chill. Gus took the little kitten with him to his house. Gus cooked bits of fish for the kitten. The kitten was very happy and took a nap in Gus's lap.

☐	Gus cooked bits of fish for the kitten.
☐	Gus took the wet kitten to his house.
☐	The kitten took a nap and was happy.
1	Gus looked at a wet kitten in a ditch.

48.   Pam did not have her school books with her. She ran back to school to get them from her room. The school was locked and Pam was sad. Then Pam ran into Ms. Cook as she looked into the locked school. Ms. Cook let Pam into the school to get her books. Pam ran to her room, tucked her books into her sack, and ran back to Ms. Cook.

☐	Ms. Cook let Pam into the school.
☐	Pam tucked her books into her sack.
☐	Pam ran into Ms. Cook.
1	Pam ran back to the school.

49. Jan was _____ her bike.

   fix   fixing

50. Dan's jacket had a _____ in it.

   rip   ripped

51. Rags can _____ for bits of ham.

   beg   begged

52. Grandma is _____ for Nat in the shed.

   check   checking

1. band
   bent
   dent

2. last
   fist
   fast

3. bank
   melt
   belt

4. pest
   best
   past

5. here
   house
   home

6. dad
   day
   play

7. dot
   doll
   dog

8. here
   her
   were

9. lunchroom
   bathroom
   bedroom

10. hitting
    helping
    humming

11. lists
    lifts
    lips

12. sill
    sell
    shell

13. _____

14. _____

15. _____

16. _____

17.   Pam went to run and play in the sand. She began by playing with a pan, and then she made a sunfish in the sand. Pam had a very good day playing in the sand. When she looked at the sunset, she had to go home for dinner.

Pam made a sunfish in the sand.
Pam had fun playing in the sand.
Pam looked at the sunset and went home.

18. Pam made a _____ .

sunset

sunfish

pan

19.   Jim went shopping for a gift for his mom. He went to a shop that had things his mom likes. His mom is fond of vests, so he got her a vest. Jim had the man at the shop pack the vest in a gift box with a ribbon on it. He took the gift home and hid it in his room.

Jim got a gift for his mom.
Jim had a ribbon on the gift.
Jim hid the gift in his room.

20.   Jim looked _____ .

for his mom

in a shop

in his room

21.   Dad and Dan met a man with lots of things to sell. He was sitting by the pond as they were passing by. He had maps, mops, socks, and pots in a big sack on his back. Dad got ten maps from the man and Dan got socks. After the man handed the things to Dad and Dan, he set his pack on a bench and rested by the pond.

> Dad and Dan met a man sitting by a
> pond who had lots of things to sell.
> The man rested by the pond.
> Dad got ten maps from a man who
> had lots of things to sell.

22. Dad got _____ .

> ten maps
> ten socks
> ten pots

23.   Grandma set up the tent for Pam and Kim to nap in, but a big wind lifted the tent. Grandma went to the woodshed for bits of wood to fix the tent. She cut ten wooden pegs to hit into the tent. After Grandma fixed the tent, she zipped it up and Pam and Kim were happy.

Grandma went to the woodshed for bits of wood.

Grandma zipped up the tent after it was fixed.

Grandma set up the tent for Pam and Kim.

24. A big wind _____ .

hit the pegs

hit the woodshed

lifted the tent

25. room   went   Mills's   to   Mr.   Jan

———————————————————————

26. silk   made   Tam   belts   and   felt

———————————————————————

123

27. math   tests   the   checked   boys   the

_____

28. puppy   ribbons   likes   playing   Tam's   with

_____

pot   tablets   sink   band   chest   bank

29. _____   30. _____   31. _____

32. _____   33. _____   34. _____

35. _____   36. _____   37. _____

38. _____   39. _____   40. _____

125

41. Gus and Pam like trips in the van. The van will not run. They _____.

> are happy
>
> will not go on a trip
>
> sing a song

42. Tam got on a wooden horse. She ripped her pants. Tam _____.

> will sing a song
>
> will have some milk
>
> will fix the rip

43. Pam fell and cut her leg. If her dad will help her, he will _____.

> set a pad on the cut
>
> have a nap
>
> run and play

44. Jan and Dan like to fish. They took hooks and rods to the pond. They _____.

> had fish for dinner
>
> had the mumps
>
> did a math test

45. The robin got into its nest and tucked its wings back. Then the robin looked at a bug sitting on a log by the nest. The bug looked good to the robin, so it pecked at the bug. The robin missed the bug, and the bug ran into the log.

☐	The robin tucked its wings back.
☐	The robin pecked at the bug.
1	The robin got into the nest.
☐	The bug ran into the log.
☐	The robin missed the bug.

46. Tom had a rash on his hand that itched a lot. He went to the doctor. The doctor looked at his hand and then set a pad on the rash. "Your rash is going to get well fast, Tom," said the doctor. Tom felt better and got a cab to go home.

☐	Tom went to the doctor.
1	Tom had a rash.
☐	Tom felt better very fast.
☐	The doctor looked at the hand.
☐	The doctor set a pad on the rash.

47.   Rags got up on Jan's cot to take a nap. Nat jumped up on the cot with Rags for a nap. Nat licked his legs and then began to lick Rags's leg. Rags's leg got very wet, and it made her mad. She jumped from the cot and ran to the bedroom and hid.

1	Nat got up on the cot.
	Rags jumped from the cot and ran.
	Nat licked Rags's leg.
	Rags got mad.
	Rags hid in the bedroom.

48.   Jan cut her hand and had to ask Dan to help her do things. He had to get her tablet and pen for school. He had to hand her books to her, tuck her lunch into her backpack, and zip her jacket. Jan was very happy Dan helped her.

	Jan asked Dan for help.
	Dan zipped Jan's jacket.
1	Jan cut her hand.
	Jan was very happy.
	Dan got her tablet and pen.

49. Gus _____ his red rash.

      rubbed   rubbing

50. Nat _____ on Ms. Cook's lap.

      jumped   jumping

51. Pam _____ Gus mop the van.

      helped   helping

52. Dan was _____ up the bits of wood.

        picked   picking

Merrill Reading Program

NAME _____

OBJECTIVE	MASTERY SCORES	NUMBER OF CORRECT RESPONSES			
		PART 1	M*	PART 2	M*
DATE OF TESTING					
WORD RECOGNITION 1. Decode pattern words	3				
2. Recognize sight words	3				
3. Recognize applications of patterning	3				
ENCODING 4. Write dictated words	3				
COMPREHENSION 5. Identify details	3				
6. Identify the main idea	3				
7. Identify words to form sentences	3				
8 Identify multiple meanings	9				
9. Draw conclusions	3				
10. Sequence events	3				
11. Use inflectional endings	3				
TOTAL:		/52	/11	/52	/11

M*   If the number of correct items meets or exceeds the mastery score, place a ✔ in the box to indicate that the objective has been mastered.